A Love that Lives Beneath the Skin

Athena Ballard

BookLeaf Publishing

India | USA | UK

Presentation by *BookLeaf Publishing*

Web: www.bookleafpub.com

E-mail: info@bookleafpub.com

ISBN: 9789358317749

First edition 2023

To L.B.,

Thanks for keeping my ego in check.

LOVE LETTERS FROM THE DEEP

they find each other in the darkest reaches. there's no
sun
down here, except for her, cleaving through the sea
　　　like something worth running from.
he orbits her for a while, his pathetic wriggling body
soft against hers. a first touch that lasts forever.
(i want to kiss you. i want to eat you. i don't care,
as long as we're together.) he's only eaten
once or twice in his entire life, and she tastes
like fruit, bleeding moonlight into his mouth.
it's a love deeper than hunger, a love she can feel,
writhing in her guts. he gives up every thought,
every organ, commits himself to the flesh of her side.
they'll share this body forever. the best things end
in total darkness—the last thing he sees
are her sightless eyes. a lamp that hangs
　　　high above her head like an angel.
she wears what's left of him like a medal,
a graveyard that swims. her children will remember
　　　how his mouth filled with want.
half of them will be just as lucky.

VACANCY

I just want to see you. To love you with my eyes
open.
I know you from the neck down, every freckle,
every scar,
but that's where you end. I imagine your eyes
would be blue or brown or grey, or green
like the teeth of a flesh-eating flower.
You hang your coat at the door but you won't
let me see you. Let me kiss the mouth that says
it loves me.
Let me know you like a light switch in a dark
room.
You guide my fingers over the latch. The mask
slips out of my hands. I want to crush it.
I want to put it back. (I see you.)
I drink in the sight. It goes down bitter. You are
nothing like I imagined. My hands map your
face,
your jaw, your nose. You're not even smiling.
Your eyes catch a sliver of light, like a bird
caught in an oil slick. A color I can hardly name.
You had nothing to hide. I watch you unravel in
my hands,
coming apart like so much shining yarn.

BURNOUT

Everything is made to break. Like pulling
on a fraying sweater. He knows he isn't special.
He can only hope that something is left of him.
(Denial, 1944. Acrylic on canvas. A formal self
portrait.)
Someday they'll discover him. Most geniuses died
poor.
Each piece is senseless, spinning out of control—
      —an artist sprawled in a smoking crater.
(Anger, 1945. Ink on paper. A broken window.)
It's not like he can do anything else. His hands
are useless at every trade. He can hardly
raise a cup to his lips. But he can still paint.
(Bargaining, 1945. Oil on canvas. A symphony
          of surgical instruments.)
    Nothing works. Nobody visits.
What good is pain without purpose?
He fills the empty space with more art.
(Depression, 1946. Graphite on wove paper.
    An empty easel.)
His last painting now collects dust
    in an attic somewhere.
He'd roll in his grave at the thought, if there was
a body to bury. (Acceptance, 1946. Acrylic on
canvas.

    A dandelion, and a very strong wind.)

PET RAT

If love were a feeling, it would be a beloved pet rat
dining on my insides (I might name him
Crackers).
He doesn't want to be there, always pacing,
claws skating over my ribs. He would start
small—
lungs, liver, a kidney or two—saving the best
bits
for last. He feasts on my heart over several days,
        and then whatever's left,
tunneling through me to reach you.

I'd offer up that rat, plump and bloody,
just to catch your eye. Maybe you had one too,
the Cheese to my Crackers, a greedy little thing
climbing up the ladder of your spine.
Maybe they'll get along. Maybe we could trade.
But then there's a chance I'll find him belly up,
sick and starved from your neglect.
        I think I'll keep him to myself.

HAND STITCHED

She comes in through the window again,
having smashed the lock. He finds her sitting
      on the bed, full of half-hearted sorries
for tracking mud on the carpet. She holds her hand
out,
as though to shake—he takes it, squeezes just
      once. Blood gushes between their fingers.
He makes quick work of the wound, sewing it up
and kissing her palm, instead of apologizing.
Her knuckles are littered with scars (bar fights,
 he always assumed) and today he finds a few more:
      A deep incision across her ribcage, and
      A chunk of flesh torn loose from her shoulder
        (an arrow, she says, all matter-of-fact), and
      A ring of jagged holes punched into her ankle.
He's always exceedingly thorough, and if she notices
that he's dragging it out, she doesn't say anything.
She just complains about his bedside manner
(smiling as she does it). She always says thank you.
      Her voice has a distinct quality to it:
hoarse, crackling, like she'd swallowed an entire
campfire.
She says his name like the rasp of a knife upon stone.
She doesn't say goodbye. Tomorrow night,
      he'll leave the window open.

BROKEN TOOTH

You're sitting in a car with something broken.
You can't fix it. You can't get rid of it.
You tape it together and say a couple words,
like a band-aid on a broken wrist.
You can't remember if it was ever whole. There was
a day suffused in watercolor haze, red around
the edges
like a fresh tattoo. It wasn't broken then.

You want a love like being baptized, like someone's
holding your head under water until you thrash,
gasping out another name. Instead, you have
a cornered animal kicked one too many times.
A bitten hand, a broken mirror. It wants so badly
to be taken care of, to sink into a set of hands,
but knows better than that. People can kick.

You were fraught with something familiar (but you knew
to treat it like a tumor), something that sounded
like an echo, something that smiled with all its teeth
and put its elbows up on the table and said

I want more than this. I want to exist.
You buried its body every night, and every
morning
there it was, sleeping soundly beside you.

You're lying awake with something broken.
You won't fix it. You won't get rid of it.
You'll pick at the scab like a man twice divorced
rubbing that pale ring below the knuckle,
wishing
it was a scar. You'll be chasing that feeling
for the rest of your life, saying over and over:
        this time will be different.

A SEER AND A THIEF

thief is in seer's shop tonight, hands behind thief's back,
reading off the names of seer's tea collection
(disobey time. morning moonfizz. echinacaea.),
hoping a voice might drown out the sound
of priceless crystals falling into thief's pockets.
(citrus punch. eldritch madness. tomato mint.)
seer thinks thief is pretty—pretty for someone
whose face is never seen, only felt,
grains of stubble interpreted like writing on a wall—
—very pretty, but very dense. a cat who kept falling,
a cat who kept landing. thief had a bad habit of
outwitting fate; it almost makes seer believe in luck.
tonight, seer turns a blind eye (as though seer
had any other eye to turn). thief stares into those eyes
as though thief could climb inside (an open hatch,
an open window) and slip seer's sight into thief's pocket;
seer could be richer than God if seer wanted to be.
it would be wonderful, thief says, to look out
into the sky and see not just tonight's stars, but
tomorrow's.
when seer looks into the sky, there are no stars.
the moon tells seer that tomorrow, thief's sticky hands
will
find themselves in shackles. warden's keys will be
hanging on a hook, catching the light of the sun.
thief will come back in a few months, with a new name
and a new career. seer won't know the difference.

BROUGHT TO HEEL

You wanted me so badly, almost
like a dog at the door, waiting to come in.
You held your glass between both hands, tightly
    (so you wouldn't be tempted to touch me).

A dog at the door, begging for permission
I have a strict no strays policy and I'm
    allergic, anyways, but for you—
    —just this once.

    We could be textbook,
the two of us on a checkered blanket.
    I'd say let's get a coffee and
    you'd smile without an ounce of pity.

Dinner and a movie, and I'd get to choose—just
as long as
it's not horror (I know you're squeamish).
You'd hold the door like a gentleman. And I'd
stumble
    over those three little words, that I—

—it's not easy to love a corpse.
I'm no better than a butcher's scraps
(not that you mind, you eat like a man starved,
    what's another empty meal?)

I say don't follow me. You don't listen.
But you also don't scream when I pop the trunk.
You hold the shovel like a gentleman,
        and I say: thank you. That's all.

In the morning, I find more evidence of us:
        your jacket on the couch,
my shirt on the chair—each button undone
        with a surgeon's precision.

There's parts of you and parts of me,
        spread across the floor like
        some kind of crime scene;
we're Adam and Eve in a bed of apple seeds.

My attacker drops like a rock, gaping with
wounds.
        A hack job, if I'm being honest,
but it's you doing it, holding that knife with
your own two hands (I didn't even put it there.)

You look like a pet surrounded by shredded
pillows—
—so well trained. My very own guard dog.
My palm fits neatly under your chin, thumb
tracing
the slope of your jaw—beneath the skin,

        I can feel your teeth.

OH, POSSUM

She sleeps on the side of the road,
breathless and still, but her body is warm.
      Maybe she's faking it.
      Who can say?
Schrodinger's possum in an endless nap,
inspiring flies as cars pass by.
The pouch has always been their safehouse,
a second womb, but in her death—
      —a cradle becomes a coffin.
The first of them is born again
frail and beady-eyed, treading softly
from the scene of the crime.
He finds a familiar face
curled up in a graveyard of stars;
her mottled surface is as welcoming
      as his mother's side.

DINNER BELL

I watch the red streak along the column
of your throat—it moves as you swallow.
I soaked your hands in coppery viscera, spilling
blood and gore on our wedding bed.
Your touch, so tender as you dug through my
guts,
clever hands searching for pomegranate seeds.
Soon you'll be begging for one more bite.
You make me feel like something worth
savoring.
You cut away another piece of me, red and raw
(I prefer it well done). I can hardly keep it down.
You work my jaw in slow circles, a pale
imitation
of chewing. Your eyes seem hungrier when
they're
watching me, even now, my prime cuts
silver plattered just for you.
It tastes much better when you kiss me—
    —such a messy eater.

A NEW LIFE IS LIKE A CRIME SCENE

A: A Second Chance: a shining gun, beaten up like a
    beloved stuffed animal. There are better ways
    to reinvent yourself, but this is easier.

B. A Gamble: an outstretched hand.
    All human beings have the urge
    to take care of something.

C. A Message: a book. Given as a gift,
    returned with a few pages folded over.
    What else do they have to talk about?

D. A Lie: a cracked gas mask. Origin unknown.
    Clinging to an illusion of identity.

E. A Tool of Self Destruction: an outstretched hand,
    again. Thoroughly bitten by stray dogs.
    Some people are too far gone.

F. A Memory: a shared cigarette. Two sets
    of fingerprints. The smoke
    frames your face like a bridal veil.

G. A Declaration of Love: three broken ribs.
    Love is taking a bullet (or two, or three)
    for someone who doesn't deserve it.

H. A Fantasy: a shining gun, again.
    There's only one way to pay off
    a life debt. What do you say
    when someone saves you?

I. A Promise: a bottle of champagne. You always said
    you'd open it when the world ended.
    Love is letting someone else pour the drinks.

J. A Fresh Start: a name. We did this whole thing
    backwards. Still, it's nice to meet you.

CURTAIN CALL

It's not like me to miss my cue,
but the sight of you leaves me
somewhat brainless (I could spend
a lifetime like that, waiting in the wings,
counting acts till we were alone backstage).
You, soaking up the spotlight, casting
such a comfortable shadow. I go blank.
You're always telling me to improvise,
to say it on the spot, but I know your lines
better than mine, watched the words take flight
        from their pillowy roost.
Loving you is like putting on an act;
the two of us falling into step. When you
hold my face, it leaves a mark,
like smeared sharpie on your palms:
a kiss that says "I was here."
There we were, playing our part,
a hero and a lovestruck fool.
This role suits you (as for mine,
I can't complain). You're too good at this.
        Almost like you mean it.
You look at me like you've written your lines
        on the corner of my mouth;
you don't just say my name,
you deliver it like a prayer, a promise,

a farewell for shrikes flying south.
I want you to say it again,
        once more, with passion.
We could dance like this for hours,
long after the spotlight goes dim
like a sky surrenders to night.

TWIN SIZED COFFIN

We sleep in the same grave, pressed together
like lovers—that'd be nice, wouldn't it?
Star-crossed lovers, made for each other, instead
of
     two loose ends tied together.
Why dig two graves when one will do?
It's been 4 hours/months/days when
you tell me you love me. I tell you
that you're wrong. We are all that's left
of each other. Just because you're stuck with
me—
"Stockholm syndrome," you say, "That's what it
is."
     So now I'm your kidnapper?
You lean in closer—I'd feel your breath on my
face,
     if you could breathe, and you say,
       "Who said it's you?"
We split custody of the insects—they
crawl out of your wounds and back into mine.
We age like milk. I do, anyway.
You look as good as the day you died.
It's been 10 minutes/weeks/years when
I remember that you killed me. You ask me
     if that really matters, right now.

I suppose it doesn't. A king-sized coffin
might as well be empty: me and my bones
and a big hole in the ground. And besides,
        I don't like sleeping alone.

BUTTERFLIED

Cynthia was going to jump. I'd been trying to talk her down
for hours. I'd only known her for that long. She's almost
a stranger to me. I might've met her. Might've traded smiles in the
stairwell.
I just couldn't attach a face to that name. Had I ever met a
Cynthia?
She lived here, she was on the roof, and she
was going to jump (seven floors. Can a person survive that?)
    Butterfly (noun): a nectar feeding insect.

I watch her fall past my window.
She casts the room in psychedelic hues, her sweeping wings
thin enough for the city lights to seep through.
My room becomes a solar system, a galaxy, utterly awash
in Cynthia and her jewel tones. The world goes dark again
    Surreal (adjective): marked by the intense irrational reality
of a dream.

I have to look. It would only be a moment—
—the final chapter of Cynthia before the book closes.
I expect to see a mattress, a TV crew,
a girl grinning up at me–I expect to be played.
    Metamorphosis (noun): a striking change in circumstances.

Instead, I see her. I see her. Cynthia, Cynthia, Cynthia, spread out
on the pavement like jelly on bread. She's hardly a person
anymore.
There's the faintest shape of something, chalk at a murder scene,
but Cynthia is so scrambled that I cannot separate meat
from bone, blood from brain. I now understand why cocoons are
closed.
    Butterfly (verb): to split almost entirely and spread apart.

LOVE AT FIRST FIGHT

You say my name like
        some kind of threat.
    Just once, I want you to mean it.
I could be your sword, your attack dog,
a faithful shadow hanging off of your heel.
When you see me (when I see you),
my heart moves like a moth in a corridor,
        spinning towards certain death.
Call it a truce or call it a surrender, as long
        as I can call you mine.
I think I could live in the space
between your armor and your body
(soaking up those fatal blows) and I still
wouldn't be close enough.
        You say my name like
            you hate the taste of it.
I find sonnets in every syllable, love songs
crawling in the back of your mouth.
Your knife sings so sweetly as it sinks
        into my back;
you've wounded me, my dear,
        and the worst part is that
            you won't do it again.

EROSION

Rain came down for the first time
    when the earth met the tide.
He didn't like this fierce new god
gleefully carving canyons through the land.
A flood feels like an open wound—the sea god digs
her fingers in. Some are distant aches, a deep canal
cutting quietly across the earth, or vicious streams
to steal his favorite creatures. Their bodies are dashed
against the rocks, and what remains is swept into
the sea.
The earth god, rooted to the spot, can only watch
from afar, envious. He wishes she was gentler with him.
It's not fair that such a brutal god could be so
beautiful.
He envies drowning sailors, who could delight
in this feeling forever. He sees his own prying eyes
reflected in the nape of her neck. The sea god smiles,
all soft coral tones, caresses the earth with a touch
like sea foam. What a wonderful way to be unmade.
The earth god gives up, gives in;
    sand and silt are soon to follow.

AUTUMN AUTOPSY

Let's carve pumpkins together—
we could be raking leaves or picking apples
but I want nothing more
than to drench my clothes in pumpkin guts.
We share the same knife, a flimsy plastic thing
that couldn't cut through a sheet of paper.
I'll be scrubbing this texture off my hands for
hours
(I'll be scraping it off the walls for even longer).
It was your idea to get the kitchen knife.
Pumpkin flesh or human flesh, a knife
doesn't know the difference and now
your hands are soaked in blood and
pumpkin guts (I think I see a sliver of bone),
	red and orange and white like
so much candy corn. My car is a mess
	from last week's hayride (I see you in
the rearview, picking straw out of your wound).
They're playing Christmas music on the radio.
I sit in the emergency room with terracotta
palms,
		waiting for winter.

STELLAR COLLISION

Do you think our atoms ever touched?
In the cold quiet of space, we might've
circled each other like sharks.
We might've shared the same star, or
maybe we were neighbors, when the
Milky Way tore into existence.
We might've seen the first sunrise.
(We might've BEEN the first sunrise).
We might've been the first fish, cutting
through that cold blue abyss. We might've been
the first birds, singing together
before we knew what music was.
I feel like I've met you a million times,
watching you through foggy glass like
       an atom inside of a star.
Would you notice if you lost something
from six or seven lifetimes ago?
Maybe we'll meet again next time around:
a stellar collision and a spilled drink.
Maybe we'll do things properly, or maybe
we'll scatter, drifting across galaxies
like so many minnows—in pieces again
and again. Every particle of me
still seeks you out. Maybe
      we'll finally touch.

LOST AND FOUND

i. twenty twelve. his tour guide doesn't speak a
lick of greek.
she asks to see his watch, two fingers turning the
knobs
(the other two ghosting over his pulse point). she
sets it
three hours ahead, tells him that it's good to be
on time.
her eyes are whiskey dark, a flash of gold like
the wedding ring
that he'll turn his hotel room inside out trying to
find.

ii. nineteen twenty four. He's cleaning cups when
she walks in.
she pays double for every drink, so he looks
away
when her hand ends up in a purse or a pocket.
hanging from
her neck is her newest prize, a brassy pendant
in the shape of a spider. he steals a glance at her
pale throat,
where her collarbones meet like the hands of a
clock.

iii. sixteen fifty five. she's precious cargo
tonight.
the shackles don't stop her from reaching for his
hands, begging
for one more heist. he obliges her, at first. a kiss
through a cage.
a dropped key. she's gone in a blink, leaves him
feeling
several pounds lighter. he knows she'll walk to
death row singing.
she'll die with his heart in her back pocket.

iv. twenty twenty three. his flight attendant is
flirting with him.
she knows his name without asking. he knows
her too;
he's been batting her hands away for hundreds
of years.
she remembers how he likes his coffee. the plane
lands
three hours early—he'll find her phone number
in his back pocket,
      right where his wallet used to be.

PSYCHOSIS

Love and lust used to be twins
threaded from the same weave:
so when Psyche stole that first glance
at Eros, knife in hand, did she feel either?
She set into the dark expecting a monster,
        a fight for survival, and instead
found Cupid curled up in her bed.
Maybe she was pleasantly surprised, or
disappointed—she'd been looking forward
to the monster. Maybe it didn't matter to her.
Maybe she just wanted him to say her name
like he always said it, low and sweet—to see
the shape of each letter on his pretty lips.
They always spoke in whispers, as quiet
        as the hiss of hot oil upon pale flesh.
        Eros wore that burn for weeks
like it was a birthmark. A token of her affection.
He was obsessed with it, the artful splash
that framed his face like scattered kisses.

JANE DOE

I still remember that feeling, falling into your trap.
I could not find the strength (or urge) to look away,
blinded by something primal. Your paths were senseless,
cutting through rivers and crawling through bramble—
　　—it's like you were running from something.

I'll never forget how you looked (or how you smelled,
or how you'd taste)
or how long you stared down the nose of my gun,
at the two barrels, side by side like a pair of wedding
rings.
I clung to you like oil on fur (you didn't make it easy,
　　　but I liked that too).

I carried you home, unwound the rope from your ankles,
buried you in my nest until I could hardly find
your spidery limbs among the twigs and leaves.
I fed you with my own two hands (even when you bit
me). Tell me,
　　　isn't that love? Don't you think so?

You were so cold, immune to my charms, until you
weren't,
softened like sea glass worn down by the waves.
Now I could hold my prize catch without her shaking.
　　　Like that picture of us on the wall—my hand
in your hair, my coat on your shoulders. You were
nearly smiling.